CW00530314

THE ADVENTU
CHARLIE

Godders

Illustrated by:

Natalie and Talisha France

BOOK 3.

The Magpies Treasure

Charlie considered himself to be one extremely fortunate cat.

He and his brother Chester had been unwanted and unloved, that is, apart from the care always shown to them at the cats home.

They spent every day inside wire cages, never seeing the outside world.

But everything had changed for the brothers when, totally unexpected, they had been taken to live in a large house in the countryside.

Their new house had lots of grass, where they could play and next door there was a large field in which they had many of their adventures

There were Sheep, Pigs, Rabbits, a Pond, and lots of Birds in the field, and the two Cats found plenty to do every day.

This is Charlie`s story Part three.

After the excitement of the fishing trip, when Thomasina had fallen into the pond, and of course the Piggies mess incident, Charlie was very keen to take her to meet his other friends, and for them to play games together in the field.

Every day he went to his garden fence and peered through the thick hedgerow, but that annoying cat was nowhere to be seen.

Charlie knew that Thomasina had been very dirty and smelly after falling into the Piggies muck, and that her owner was quite angry with her, even blaming him for Thomasina`s clumsiness, which of course was very unfair. It now seemed that the silly cat had been banned from coming out to play with him, and Charlie had almost given up hope of ever seeing her again.

Then, one morning, as he peeped through the bushes that made up the hedge, there she was, sitting on the neighbours garden bench washing herself, so Charlie squeezed himself through the tiny opening, padded acrosss the grass, and sat down.

"Hello Tom" said Charlie, " Are you going to come through the hedge and play with me, we can have another adventure".

Thomasina turned her head and looked at Charlie.

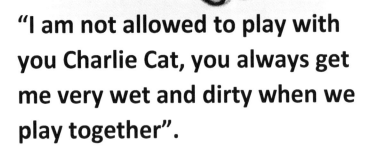

"I am not allowed to play with you Charlie Cat, you always get me very wet and dirty when we play together".

"But it is simply not my fault that you are so clumsy" grinned Charlie, "and in any case, we can always play games that do not have mud or water in them".

"You promised that I would not get dirty, when we played out the last time" sniffed Thomasina. "But my owner was furious with me because of the Piggies muck, and now I have to wear a pink bow around my neck, to remind me that girl`s are not supposed to get themselves wet and muddy".

"I cannot be blamed for your clumsiness, but, I do promise that there is not any water or mud, where Mr Magpie lives" said Charlie, as Thomasina climbed down from the bench and sat next to him.

"I do not know if that is such a good idea, Charlie cat" said Thomasina. "I do like playing with you, and your friends, but I always get dirty, which upsets my owner".

"Trust me" smiled Charlie, "Mr Magpie does not like getting wet or dirty either, it will be fun"

"Well if you absolutely do promise not to get me dirty, I suppose that it might be fun" purred Thomasina.

"That's what I have been saying" chuckled Charlie, as he stood up, "Now do come along Tom, you are such a slow cat". And he pushed himself back through the small gap in the garden hedgerow, followed somewhat reluctantly, by the much larger Thomasina.

The two cats padded across Charlies garden, and through the fence at the other side, which put them in the field.

Once again they went past the fishing pond, and Thomasina could not help remembering that she had fallen into the water.

They walked past two of the sheep, who said, "Baa Baa, Hello Charlie and Thomasina".

This time however, they did not go through the second hedge, instead, Charlie led the way across the field to the far corner, where a large tree had fallen down.

The tree was not dead, its roots were still firmly in the grassy bank, and lots of new branches and twigs sprouted outwards.

Suddenly there was a loud chattering noise, and a big black bird flew over their heads and landed on the tree trunk.

"Caw Caw Charlie" said the bird, "Who have you bought with you"?.

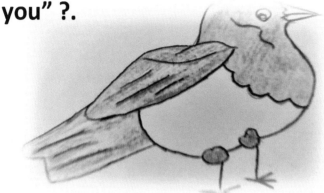

"Hello to you Mr Magpie"replied Charlie, "I want you to meet Big Tom, he is my new friend, he lives in the house next door to us".

"Well then, I am very pleased to meet you Tom" said the Magpie, I do hope that you are not one of those cats that like to chase birds".

"Why would a cat wish to chase a bird"? asked Thomasina.

"Caw, Caw, Caw" laughed the Magpie, "where did you find your friend Charlie, he does not know much about the countryside, and how we live".

"He is from a town Mr Magpie" said Charlie, "I think that people must live differently in towns and cities".

"For your information, I am a real cat, and can talk, just like

you Mr Magpie" hissed
Thomasina, "and if all Birds are
so rude to cats, I can easily
understand why they wish to
chase them away".

"And, my name is NOT Big Tom,
but Thomasina, and I am a Girl
Cat, if you look, my pink bow,
might have helped you with that
understanding".

"Oh pardon me, little Miss Kitty
Cat, Charlie and me are sorry
that we are simple country
dwellers" chuckled Mr Magpie.

"I know that your proper name
is not Big Tom" smiled Charlie,
"but you are a big cat, and I
think that Thomasina is silly, we
play together, so it does not

matter whether we are Boy or Girl, if we are friends".

"Cats do not chase Birds because of what they say" crowed Mr Magpie, "It is what cats are supposed to do, but Charlie and me are best friends, so things are different for us".

"I do not want to chase you either", said Thomasina, " so we can be friends too".

"Can we see your treasure store please Mr Magpie"? said Charlie.

"Caw Caw, of course" replied the Magpie, and it hopped down from the tree trunk and wobbled across the ground to a small hollow in the side of the tree.

Charlie and Thomasina followed, and as the Magpie stood to one side, they peered at the pile of bright shiny objects laid in the soft birds nest.

There was a silvery ring pull from a can of drink, some shiny tin foil wrappers from sweets, several very brightly coloured buttons of different sizes and shapes, a gold colour hair slide, a dented thimble, and a silver 5 pence coin. But, what made Thomasina stare, was the sparkling gold ring, that Mr Magpie held up.

"Do you like my collection"
asked Mr Magpie, "It has taken a
Long time to gather each
item".

"It is quite amazing" said
Thomasina quietly, then pulling
Charlie to one side, she hissed,
"That ring, belongs to my owner,
she is so worried about losing it"

"What do you want me to do"
asked Charlie, "the Magpie is my
friend, and if he has taken your

owners ring, then it is her fault, for leaving it laying out on show".

"I really do not like you sometimes, Charlie cat" hissed Thomasina, "You can be very rude and annoying". She glared at Mr Magpie and said, "Your treasure does not belong to you, everything was stolen from its rightful owner somewhere, you should be ashamed that you have taken it".

"Well now, Miss Snooty Cat", said Mr Magpie, "I only pick up what I find, if people want to throw away their things, how is that my fault" . ?

"I have changed my mind about chasing naughty birds" said Thomasina, and Hissed loudly in Mr Magpies face.

The startled Magpie, suddenly flew up into the air, squawking wildly, "Caw, Caw, Caw" it sang.

"You certainly know how to make new friends, Big Tom" chuckled Charlie, "I do hope that Mr Magpie does not blame me for your anger".

"Please take me home now Charlie" muttered Thomasina, "I do not like your friend the Magpie".

As the two cats reached the fence between their houses, Thomasina turned to Charlie and said. "You do not need to come into my garden anymore, as I will not be playing with you again".

"Whatever have I done now"? Asked Charlie, "it was you who made such a fuss, It is not my fault that Mr Magpie thinks that he is clever by taking things to decorate his nest".

"You said that it was my owners fault, for losing her ring" spat Thomasina, "You are without any doubt a horrid cat". And with that, she pushed her body into the opening.

Charlie hesitated for just a second, then followed into Thomasina`s garden.

Suddenly the door to the house opened and Thomasina`s owner was standing there, looking down at the two cats.

"Thomasina, you can be quite naughty, I told you not to play with that bad cat" she said.

Ignoring the lady`s words, Charlie padded towards her, then slowly unfolded his paw and dropped a golden ring at her feet.

The lady, stooped down and picked up the ring, turning it over in her fingers. "Oh my, what a clever cat you are Charlie" she said, "You have found my lost ring".

She bent down, scooped Charlie into her arms and carried him into the house, calling out "Come along Thomasina" .

Placing Charlie onto the kitchen floor, the lady went to one of the cupboards, took out a tin and after opening it, placed some salmon into a bowl, which she put in front of Charlie. "Here you are, you clever boy" she cooed, "you can play with Thomasina whenever you want". After eating all of the fish, Charlie purred his thanks, then turning towards Big Tom, who was sitting by the door scowling, said. " It is time for me to go home now, but we can play again soon".

And he scampered out of the house and back through the hedgerow. At home Charlie was surprised that his bowl was on its own, and Chester`s was nowhere to be seen. After eating his tea, he wandered around the house, but Chester was not to be found anywhere, and after climbing into his comfy bed he was soon sound asleep.

The following morning there was still no sign of his brother, and no food bowl with Chesters name on it.

After eating his breakfast, Charlie searched everywhere but Chester was simply nowhere to be found.

He meowed loudly in front of his owner, several times, and was picked up and cuddled.

"Your brother is not with us anymore", she said.

Then wiping a tear from her eyes, continued.

"Just this side of heaven, you can find the Rainbow Bridge Charlie, it is a wonderful place where special animals, like you and Chester go when they pass away. It is full of meadows, hills, streams and flowers, and the animals live there, and play together happily for ever, Chester has gone to live there".

Charlie was very sad about his brother going away, but he liked the idea of him playing with other animals, and guessed that one day, he would join them.

For several days, he sat on his tree stump, waiting for Thomasina to come out and play, but even when the stars and Moon came out to shine, she was nowhere to be seen.

Then one sunny morning, as Charlie was lying in the sunshine she suddenly appeared in Charlies garden.

"Hello Big Tom" said Charlie, " I have been patiently watching out for you".

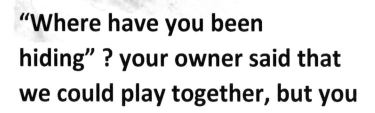

"Where have you been hiding" ? your owner said that we could play together, but you have not been out since we found her ring".

"It was me, not we, who found her ring" hissed Thomasina, "and yet you get the fresh Salmon and all of the praise, it is so unfair".

"But it was me who took it from Mr Magpie, and carried it home for your owner" cried Charlie, "You were happy to leave it there".

"Well, I still think that it is not fair" said Thomasina, "but I do like you Charlie Cat, so I am willing to play with you again".

"Oh goody" replied Charlie, "we can go to the field and see the sheep".

The two cats padded across the grass, through the hedge into the field, and Charlie led the way to where the sheep lived.

"Baa Baa Charlie" they cried as the Cats came into view, "Baa Baa Thomasina".

"Hello Sheep", said Charlie And Thomasina together, " As it is a nice sunny day we have come to play with you".

Charlie looked across the field, and saw that the gate had been left open.

"Do you want to come on an adventure sheep" ? asked Charlie.

"Baa, Baa, Baa", the Sheep replied, and they followed Charlie and Thomasina across the field, out of the gate and along the lane.

When they reached Charlies house, he led them down the path, and round to the back garden, where there were lots of flowers and fruit growing.

Charlie laid himself down on the grass, and Thomasina sat next to him. The sheep wandered around the garden, biting at the flowers, and eating the tomatoes, raspberries and lettuces.

Suddenly the door into the house opened and Charlies owner and her daughter came out, waving their arms.

"Go away sheep" they shouted, and herded the small flock down the pathway and out of the garden gate.

"Well, it seems that my owners are not keen for our sheep friends to play in the garden", said Charlie, as he stood up.

"It is time for my tea now Big Tom, so I will see you tomorrow perhaps we can have another adventure". And with that he padded away into the house.

Nothing much happened for a few days, as Charlie and Thomasina played together, they went to see the rabbits again, and Thomasina watched as Charlie caught a fish, although this time she kept well away from the water.

Then one day when the two cats were playing in Charlies garden, several cars pulled into the driveway, and the owners children and grandchildren climbed out.

It was obviously going to be a party of somekind, as there were balloons, and presents. Charlie knew all of the visitors, as from time to time they each came to see his owners, but the grandchildren were always quite noisy, especially the younger ones, who ran around and shouted quite a lot.

When he was younger, this had frightened Charlie, but now he understood that children needed to do this, his owner called it "Letting of steam" and that he was quite safe. Strangely the four youngest grandchildren were all girls, and for humans they had odd names. There was Aleah, Talisha, Abigayle and Olivia, and he smiled to himself as they chased each other round the garden. Later there was some party food with cake, and

Charlie managed to get a share of chicken and ham, plus some leftover ice cream, everything considered, it was a good day.

Some weeks later, a sign appeared in the garden saying "FOR SALE", quickly followed by "SOLD" and Charlies owner started to take pictures from the

walls, ornaments were wrapped
in paper, then packed into
boxes, and after a few days,
piles of neatly stacked boxes
filled some of the rooms.

Charlie amused himself by hiding amongst the boxes, or climbing up onto a pile.

He even fell asleep on the very top of one stack, only to roll over as he dreamed, and fall off onto the floor, which not only made him wake up, but also hurt, although no damage was done.

He had heard the humans say that cats always landed on their feet when they fell, and he now considered that if that were true, it must only be when they were awake.

Quite a few months passed with the boxes not being moved or even touched, then late one afternoon, the owners family arrived with a big lorry, and started loading all of the boxes and furniture into it, until just a mattress and his bed remained.

After Charlie had eaten all of the breakfast food the following morning, he went to the garden fence and looked through into Thomasina`s home. She was sitting on the bench and looked up when she saw Charlie.
"Hello Charlie cat, you look a little sad, whatever is wrong" ?.

"I think that we are moving away Big Tom, we might not see each other again " Said Charlie.

"Oh dear" sighed Thomasina, "I will always remember you though Charlie cat, you will always be my best friend."

Just then Charlie's owner called his name, and he said goodbye to Big Tom, and padded across the grass. His owner picked him up and placed him into a cat carrying basket, which was put onto the seat in the back of her car.

"Take a last look Charlie" she said, "we are going to live in a new house".

Coming soon. Book 4.

Mr Fox (Missing)

Books in the series

1. **Thomasina Falls into The Pond**

2. A Muddy Disaster

3. **The Magpies Treasure**

4. Mr Fox (Missing)

5. Found at Last (Safe Again)

Printed in Great Britain
by Amazon

40038010R00032